DATE DUE		

Grassland Animals

By Christy Steele

Steadwell Books

Raintree Steck-Vaughn Publishers

A Harcourt Company

Austin · New York

www.raintreesteckvaughn.com

Published by Raintree Steck-Vaughn Publishers, an imprint of Steck-Vaughn Company.

Library of Congress Cataloging-in-Publication Data
Steele, Christy.
    Grassland animals / Christy Steele.
        p. cm. -- (Animals of the biomes)
    Summary: Describes the physical characteristics, behavior, adaptations, and life cycle of four grassland animals: the ring-necked pheasant, termite, wildebeest, and Komodo dragon.
    Includes bibliographical references. (p.).
    ISBN: 0-7398-5688-X (hc); 0-7398-6408-4 (pbk).
    1. Grassland animals--Juvenile literature. [1. Grassland animals.] I. Title. II. Series.

QL115.3 .S74 2002
591.74--dc21   2002069712

Printed and bound in the United States of America
1 2 3 4 5 6 7 8 9 10 WZ 05 04 03 02 01

Produced by Compass Books

Photo Acknowledgments
Comstock, cover, 1, 4, 20, 28, 30, 30, 42, 45; Chad Coppess, 8, 44; Corbis, 14, 18, 39, 40; Roger Treadwell, 11; Tom Edwards, 13; William Grenfall, 16, 44; Kjell Sandved, 23; Joe McDonald, 24; Digistock, 27; Hal Beral, 32; Mary and Lloyd McCarthy, 35, 45; Ken Lucas, 42.

Content Consultant
Dr. Sam McNaughton
BioResLabs, Syracuse University
Syracuse, NY 13202

This book supports the National Science Standards.

Contents

These wildebeests live on grasslands. Grasslands cover about 30 percent of Earth's surface.

Animals in the Grasslands

M any kinds of animals live in the grasslands biome. A biome is a large region, or area, made of communities. A **community** is a group of certain plants and animals that live in the same place.

Grasslands are wide, flat areas covered mainly with grasses and small shrubs. The two kinds of grasslands are tropical and temperate. Tropical grasslands form near the equator, an imaginary line that circles the middle of Earth. These grasslands are hot all year, with two seasons— dry and rainy. Temperate grasslands form farther from the equator. They are warm in summer and cold in winter. In temperate grasslands, it can rain or snow throughout the year.

| This map shows where the grasslands are located throughout the world.

What Lives in Grasslands?

Plants and animals that live in grasslands have adapted to live there. To adapt means a living thing changes over time to fit the conditions where it lives. For example, fires often burn parts of grasslands. Grassland plants have adapted to grow back after fires. The plant grows mostly underground. The top blade of grass may get burned, but most of the plant is safe under the ground. It begins growing again after the fire.

Many grasslands are dry and windy. Tropical grasslands receive more rain than temperate grasslands, so grasses grow taller there. Temperate climates sometimes have droughts. Plants must survive these long periods of time without rain or snow. Many grassland plants store water in their stems or leaves to use during dry times. Other plants have long roots to find water that flows underground.

Many different animals live in grasslands. Some build special homes called burrows or nests to live in. A **burrow** is a hole or tunnel an animal digs to live inside. These places protect them from the harsh weather of the grasslands.

The following chapters tell about four kinds of animals that live in grasslands. Ring-necked pheasants are birds that live in North America's prairies. Termites are insects that build huge mounds to live in. Herds of wildebeest roam throughout Africa's grasslands, looking for food and water. Komodo dragons hunt in tall grasses on Komodo Island.

This is a rooster. Roosters are about 1 foot tall and weigh up to 3.5 pounds. Hens are slightly smaller.

The Ring-Necked Pheasant

Ring-necked pheasants are chicken-like birds. Like chickens, male ring-tailed pheasants are called roosters, while females are called hens.

Adult ring-necked pheasants have long legs and short, round wings. They have long, pointed brown tails with black stripes. Each male has spurs, or long finger-like growths, on the backs of its legs.

Ring-necked pheasants are colorful. Rooster feathers can be brown, red, gold, and black. They have a shiny green-black head with red spots on their cheeks. A white ring of feathers circles their neck. This gives them the name "ring-necked." Females are not as colorful. Their feathers are a mix of brown, gray, and black.

Where Do Ring-Necked Pheasants Live?

Ring-necked pheasants live in central Asia, China, Japan, and southern Canada. They also live in many of America's states. Most ring-necked pheasants in America live on the grassland prairies of the Great Plains states.

Ring-tailed pheasants live mostly on the ground instead of in trees. They live in places where plants, such as wild grasses, grow.

Most ring-necked pheasants live in places with good cover. Cover is an area of low, thick, shrubby growth. When they are not eating, birds rest or hide in the cover during the day and roost there at night. To roost means to sleep.

How Have Ring-Necked Pheasants Adapted to Live in Grasslands?

Ring-necked pheasants have adapted to live in their grassland homes. Their plumage provides **camouflage** for the birds. Camouflage is coloring or patterns that make an animal blend in with its background. It is hard for predators, such as cats, dogs, and hawks, to see ring-necked pheasants when they are hiding. A **predator** is an animal that hunts other animals for food.

> **The coloring of this female helps her blend in with her surroundings.**

All birds lose their feathers each year and grow new feathers. This process is called molting. Ring-necked pheasants molt in the hot summer. By fall, when it is cooler, all their new feathers have grown in to keep them warm. This adaptation helps them survive in the different seasons of the temperate grasslands.

What a Ring-Necked Pheasant Eats

Ring-necked pheasants are omnivores. An **omnivore** eats both animals and plants. Plants are the most common food of ring-necked pheasants. At times, they eat snails and insects, such as potato beetles, grasshoppers, and crickets.

The kinds of food that grow in grasslands change with the different seasons. Ring-necked pheasants have adapted to eat many kinds of food. In spring and summer, they eat grasses, fruits, and the leaves of plants called forbs. They also eat insects. In fall, they eat grains and seeds left over from farm fields that have been harvested. In winter, they eat berries, nuts, and whatever else they can find.

During most of the year, ring-tailed pheasants live together in groups. They may travel around a home range of about 1 mile (1.6 km) to find food. A home range is an area where an animal usually lives or looks for food.

Ring-necked pheasants often use their sharp claws to scratch around on the ground to find food. In the winter, they try to find food in

This pheasant is eating seeds and grasses that it has found.

places that are not covered by snow. Sometimes they will dig through the snow to find food.

Ring-tailed pheasants are important to grasslands because they help some plants to grow. They do this by spreading seeds of the plants that they eat to new places. The seeds leave their bodies in their waste.

This adult ring-necked pheasant is protecting her young chick.

A Ring-Necked Pheasant's Life Cycle

In spring, ring-tailed pheasants begin mating season. From March to May, roosters pick territories. A territory is an area that an animal lives in and fights to protect. Roosters will fight any other roosters that enter their territory. During this time, they dance around beating their wings and calling. A ring-tailed pheasant's call is a loud double squawk.

Hens choose which rooster they want to mate with. One rooster may mate with up to eight different hens. They all live together in the male's territory during mating season.

After mating, females find a place in thick cover to build a nest. First, they dig a shallow hole and line it with leaves, grass, or other plants. A hen lays one light-tan egg per day. She may lay up to 20 eggs.

The hen then begins to incubate her eggs. To incubate is to sit on eggs to provide heat. After about 23 days, the chicks hatch.

Newly hatched chicks are covered in wet down. Down is soft, fluffy feathers. For the first weeks, the chicks will die if they become too cold or too wet. To protect them, the female sits on them to keep them warm. This is called brooding.

The hen feeds insects to her chicks. She stays with them until they are 8 to 12 weeks old. By this time, flight feathers have grown in to replace their down. Then the chicks can fly and are large enough to live on their own.

You can see the body sections of this termite.

The Termite

When most people think of termites, images of little bugs eating houses come into their minds. Some kinds of termites do eat people's houses and live in rotted wood. But many termites live in grasslands, far away from people.

All termites are insects. Insects have six legs and a body that is divided into three parts—the head, thorax, and **abdomen**. The thorax is between the head and the abdomen.

There are many kinds of termites, and each one looks a little different. Most termites are less than an inch long and white. Many are blind. They use two antennae on their heads to help them move around. Antennae are feelers. Some termites have wings, but most do not.

This termite is eating a fungus that is growing inside its nest.

Where Do Termites Live?

Termites live in most warm places around the world. Many kinds of termites live in the grasslands of Africa and Australia.

Termites are social insects. Social insects are friendly to each other and live together in groups. A group of termites is called a **colony**. Up to 5 million termites may live in a large colony.

Every termite in the colony has a special job to do. Each colony has one queen. A queen is larger than the other termites. Her job is to lay eggs. Worker termites build and clean the nest, grow or find food, and take care of the queen, the eggs, and the young termites.

Soldier termites fight to protect the nest from predators. Many animals, such as aardvarks and ants, will try to attack termite nests and eat the termites that live there.

What a Termite Eats

Termites are herbivores. Herbivores eat only plants. Each kind of termite eats the foods that grow where it lives. Termites that live in grasslands eat grasses, seeds, and other plants.

Some termites on grasslands grow food inside their nests. The food they grow is called **fungus**. A fungus is a plant-like living thing that feeds on rotting matter. Each fungus-growing colony has its own kind of fungus. The special fungus is found only in the colony and nowhere else in the world.

 This large mound is a termite nest in Africa.

How Have Termites Adapted to Live in Grasslands?

Termites have adapted to grasslands by building special homes to live in. Their nests may be up to 20 feet (6 m) tall. The nests protect the termites from predators, dry weather, storms, and fire.

To build a nest, worker ants use saliva and soil or clay particles. Saliva is a watery mixture made in the mouth. The workers mix their saliva with the soil and form it into rooms and tunnels. Each room is used for different things. The queen has one room in the center of the nest to herself. Eggs are in some rooms, while young termites are in others. Food is stored or grown in large rooms. Tunnels connect the rooms to each other, so the termites can move between them.

The nests help the termites grow the fungus to eat. It is often dry in the grasslands where they live, but fungus needs moisture to grow. To solve this problem, some termites dig deep tunnels that lead to underground water. This helps keep the air in their nest moist. The walls of the nest hold in the moisture so that it does not escape into the outside air.

Termites also need a certain temperature to grow fungus. As the fungus grows, it gives off heat. So that it does not become too hot, termites build tall chimneys with holes leading outside of their nest. The hot air flows out through the chimneys.

A Termite's Life Cycle

A termite has different stages to its life—egg, larva, pupa, and adult. The process of changing from stage to stage is called metamorphosis. A termite spends the first part of its life growing inside an egg. After 24 to 90 days, the egg hatches.

A young larva comes out of the egg. Larvae are small and worm-like. Worker termites feed and clean the larvae. Larvae eat and grow.

To enter the pupa stage, larvae spin cocoons. Inside these silky coverings, the larva turns into a pupa that looks like a fully formed adult termite. When the pupa is fully developed, it breaks out of its cocoon. It is then an adult and begins to do its job in the colony.

Once a year, alates hatch from the eggs. Alates are young kings and queens. The kings

FUN FACT

Once termites have left a nest, other animals move in and make it their home. The tall mounds are good for hiding inside.

Over time, plants begin growing on the nests until they form hills and thickets.

> This termite queen is so large because she is carrying many eggs.

and queens leave the nests to form new nests. They fly a short distance away. Once they land, they lose their wings. A male pairs up with a female. They dig a tunnel to live in and mate. Then, the queen starts laying eggs. Over time, the eggs hatch, and a new colony has formed. The new termites begin building a large nest.

An adult wildebeest like this one is about 4 feet (1.3 m) tall and weighs up to 600 pounds (275 kg).

The Wildebeest

The wildebeest is one of the many large grazing mammals that live in grasslands. Grazing animals feed on plants. A mammal is a warm-blooded animal with a backbone. Female mammals give birth to live young and feed them with milk from their bodies. Warm-blooded animals have a body temperature that stays the same, no matter what the temperature of the air or water around it.

The wildebeest is an African antelope with long thin legs. It has a large head with a long snout and curved horns. Its fur is brown, reddish, or tan, and it has a long, shaggy tail. Some kinds of wildebeest have whitish fur with stripe-like black or brown markings. There is long, white or black beard-like hair under their chins.

Where Do Wildebeest Live?

Wildebeests live in eastern and central Africa. Grasslands there are called savannas. Wildebeest are common animals from southern Kenya to South Africa. About one million wildebeest live in the Serengeti. This area is a large, flat plain in central Africa covered with many savanna areas.

Like termites, wildebeest are social animals. They live together in large herds. A herd of wildebeest can have from 5 to 1,000 animals in it. The number depends on the size of the area available for living and finding food.

How Have Wildebeest Adapted to Live in Grasslands?

Some wildebeest migrate. To do this, they move from place to place with the change of the seasons. Up to one million wildebeest leave the Serengeti during the dry season when it becomes hard to find food and water. They travel thousands of miles across the dry savannas of Africa until they find water and food. Then the wildebeest return to the savannas during the rainy season, when food and water are easy to find

This herd of wildebeest is beginning its long yearly migration.

again. In some places, grass grows all year round. Wildebeest living in these places do not migrate.

When herds of wildebeest travel, their hooves stir up the grassland soil. This dusty air is hard to breathe. To adapt, wildebeest have a lot of hair in their nostrils. The hair filters out the dust and soil so that they can breathe easier.

This wildebeest is eating the grass that grows on the savannas.

What a Wildebeest Eats

Wildebeest are herbivores. They eat plant leaves and the many kinds of grasses that grow on savannas. The wildebeest mostly eat newly grown grass. Their body is adapted for eating this sweet grass. Their head and mouth are specially shaped to eat short grasses that other animals cannot reach.

To find this newly growing grass, wildebeest often visit places that have recently burned. They eat the grass that is growing back after the fire.

Other times, wildebeest may travel behind other grazing animals. Some animals only eat the tops of grass. After these animals are through eating, the wildebeest moves in and eats the lower parts of the grass.

Wildebeest need a lot of water to survive. Wildebeest receive some of their water from their food. Their body soaks up moisture from the grass they eat. When grass is hard to find, wildebeest need to drink several times each day. They must live near streams, lakes, or pools of water.

> These young wildebeest are traveling next to their mother.

A Wildebeest's Life Cycle

The wildebeest mating season is called the rutting season. The rutting time depends on where the wildebeest live. In southern Africa, wildebeest mate from February to April. Wildebeest in the Serengeti mate from April to May.

During rutting season, males pick a territory. The male tries to find females to mate with. The females live with the male in his territory during rutting season. The male will fight other males that try to enter the territory. The male that wins the fight gets to mate with the females.

About eight to nine months after mating, females give birth. About 90 percent of all wildebeest are born within three weeks of each other. They are born early in the rainy season, when food is easy to find.

Newly born wildebeest can walk within three to five minutes of being born. They walk alongside their mothers. Their fathers are part of the herd, but do not help raise them. The whole herd helps protect the young. If a wildebeest senses danger, it makes an alarm call. Then the whole herd runs away.

Many predators, such as lions and hyenas, try to catch and eat young wildebeest. Many wildebeest die before they reach adulthood. They are fully grown at 3 or 4 years old. If they escape predators, they can live up to 20 years.

This is a Komodo dragon. In Indonesia, people call these lizards "oras." Ora means mouth.

The Komodo Dragon

The Komodo dragon is the largest lizard in the world. The biggest adult Komodo dragons can be up to 10 feet (3 m) long and weigh up to 300 pounds (135 kg). They have short legs with sharp, curved claws on their feet. A long tail trails after their thick body. They have a small head and a long neck covered by loose sagging skin.

Komodo dragons have thick scale-covered skin. Scales are small pieces of tough skin that help protect the body. Their skin is usually gray or light brown with red spots or other dark markings.

Komodo dragons have yellow forked tongues. A forked tongue looks like a little triangle has been cut out of its center.

Where Do Komodo Dragons Live?

Komodo dragons live only on several islands in Indonesia. Most of these lizards live on the island of Komodo. Some also live on small surrounding islands, including Rinca and Flores. Komodo dragons are excellent swimmers, and they sometimes swim from island to island.

Grasslands and scattered groups of trees cover the Komodo dragon's island home. When Komodo dragons are young, they spend a lot of time in the trees. When they get older, they live mostly on the ground.

How Have Komodo Dragons Adapted to Live in Grasslands?

Like all lizards, Komodo dragons are cold-blooded. Cold-blooded animals have a body temperature that changes depending on the outside temperature. During the day, it can become hot in grasslands. To adapt, Komodo dragons dig burrows in the mud. They rest in these shady burrows until the temperature cools.

The Komodo dragon's thick skin helps to hold in its body's moisture when it is dry. This way, it does not need to drink as much water.

> **This Komodo dragon's thick skin helps it hold in moisture.**

Komodo dragons have a special Jacobson's organ that they use to smell. This organ is like a nose inside the top of the lizard's mouth. To smell, the Komodo dragon flicks its tongue in and out of its mouth. When the tongue is outside, it picks up scents in the air. When the tongue returns to the inside of the mouth, it passes the scents to the Jacobson's organ there.

 Komodo dragons have special jaws that open very wide so that they can eat large prey.

What a Komodo Dragon Eats

Komodo dragons are carnivores. A **carnivore** eats only meat. The lizards eat different things depending on how old they are. Young Komodo dragons eat small animals, such as insects, mice, and lizards. Adult Komodo dragons eat larger animals. They prefer to eat deer, but will also eat wild pigs, snakes, birds, and goats. Komodo dragons will even eat smaller Komodo dragons and people. They also eat carrion, or the flesh of dead animals.

Komodo dragons are excellent hunters. They often catch food by waiting and hiding. When prey comes near, the Komodo dragon rushes at it. Prey is an animal that is hunted and eaten as food. If the Komodo dragon catches the prey, it bites it with its sharp teeth. This often kills the prey. If it does not, the prey may run away. Usually, the prey dies anyway. The animal becomes sick from bacteria passed on by the Komodo dragon's bite. Bacteria are very small living things that can make animals or plants sick.

Komodo dragons have a lot of bacteria in their mouths because they eat carrion, which is host to bacteria. The Komodo dragon tracks and follows the sick prey. Once the prey has died, the Komodo dragon eats it.

Komodo dragons can eat up to 80 percent of their body weight. They have special jaws that open very wide. This helps them swallow large pieces of the prey at one time.

A Komodo Dragon's Life Cycle

Komodo dragons usually live alone. They come together only to eat large prey and to mate.

Komodo dragons usually mate between May and August. The males sometimes fight over the females. When they fight, they stand on their back legs and wrestle with each other. The winning Komodo dragon throws the loser to the ground. Then the winner mates with the female.

The eggs develop inside the female for several weeks. Then, usually in September, the female digs a hole in the ground. She lays up to 30 eggs in the nest.

After seven months, the hatchling Komodo dragons break out of the eggs. They are only about 15 inches (38 cm) long. Young Komodo dragons may have green bands around their necks. They lose these markings as they grow older.

Young Komodo dragons are in great danger from predators. Birds or other grown Komodo dragons eat many of the young lizards. If they

▲ The markings of this Komodo dragon will
fade as it grows older.

live to become adults, they are top predators.
This means that fully grown Komodo dragons
do not have any natural enemies. They may live
up to 20 years.

Some African savannas are turning into desert. If this continues, wildebeest will have nowhere to live.

What Will Happen to Grassland Animals?

Grasslands provide a special home for the animals that live there. Many plants and animals that live in grasslands could not survive in other biomes.

Over time, people have begun to change grasslands. They may burn off the grass to plant crops and build farms. When this happens, grassland animals lose their homes. Food may become harder to find. Some animals may become endangered. Endangered means all of a particular kind of animal may die out in the wild.

In many places around the world, grasslands are turning into deserts. People may clear the soil of grassy plants. Without grass roots to hold the soil in place, it blows away. When this happens, the grassland slowly becomes a desert.

Komodo dragons like this one are an
endangered species.

How Are Grassland Animals Doing?

Some grassland animals have healthy
populations. A population is the total number of
an animal living in one place. Today, termites,
ring-necked pheasants, and wildebeest are not
in danger. In some places, people hunt
pheasants for food. But there are laws that limit

the number of birds they can kill. This helps keep the population healthy. A large part of the Serengeti was made a wildlife park to help protect the wildebeest that live there from hunters.

Komodo dragons are endangered. Because they live in so few places, a natural disaster, such as a tidal wave, could wash over the islands and kill them all. But people are one of the greatest dangers to their habitat. A habitat is a place where an animal or plant usually lives. As more of the islands' grasslands and forests are torn down for human activity, Komodo dragons have fewer places to live.

In some areas, hunters have killed many of the deer that Komodo dragons feed on. This is another threat to the population.

Unless people work to save the grasslands, other animals such as the ring-necked pheasant and wildebeest could also become endangered. Some people are saving grassland animals by creating national parks. It is against the law to build or hunt in these places. If we save the grasslands, the animals that live there will survive in their homes for a long time.

Quick Facts

Ring-necked pheasants first came from the grasslands  of Asia. In the 1880s, people brought the birds to the United States on boats and released them into the wild.

If a hen lays eggs and her nest is destroyed, she will build a new nest and lay more eggs. She may do this several times.

Some termites have special biting mouthparts called mandibles that are used for fighting. Mandibles move side to side like scissors instead of up and down like people's jaws do.

Wildebeest means "wild beast."

Another name for the wildebeest is gnu.

Some herds of wildebeest sleep together in rows. This makes it harder for predators to catch them.

Unlike its prey, a Komodo dragon will not become sick if another Komodo dragon bites it. Scientists are not sure why the bacteria does not make other Komodo dragons sick, too.

Glossary

abdomen (AB-duh-muhn)—the back section of an insect's body

burrow (BUR-oh)—a hole or tunnel in the ground where an animal lives

camouflage (KAM-o-flaj)—colors, shapes, and patterns that make something blend in with its background

carnivore (KAHR-nuh-vor)—an animal that eats only meat

colony (KOL-uh-nee)—a large group of living things that lives and works together

community (kuhm-YOO-nih-tee)—different species of plants and animals living together in a habitat

fungus (FUHN-guhss)—a plant-like living thing that feeds on rotting matter

omnivore (AHM-nee-vohr)—an animal that eats both plants and animals

predator (PRED-uh-tur)—an animal that hunts other animals for food

Addresses and Internet Sites

Nature Conservancy
1815 North Lynn Street
Arlington, VA 22209

Pheasants Forever
1783 Buerkle Circle
St. Paul, MN 55110

**Tallgrass Prairie National
Preserve**
P.O. Box 585
Cottonwood Falls, KS 66845

**EEK! Environmental
Education for Kids**
www.dnr.state.wi.us/org/
caer/ce/eek/index.htm

Grassland Explorer
www.naturegrid.org.uk/
grassland/index.html

Grasslands Biome
mbgnet.mobot.org/pfg/
diverse/biomes/grasslnd
/index.htm

Books to Read

**Lalley, Patrick and Lalley,
Janet**. *Grassland
Scientists*. Austin, TX:
Steck-Vaughn, 2002.

Scheff, Duncan.
Grasslands. Austin, TX:
Steck-Vaughn, 2001.

Index